Edited by Adele Pickerill

Cover, Book Design and Illustrations
by © Robert Hall and Zhuohan Shao

Contents

Introduction

If there was only one thing we could safely put a bet on - it would be that the world and businesses we work in, will continue to go through complex change.

One of the reasons for that change is the impact of digital transformation (or as it's been described digital disruption), not only on the technology and systems we use, but on how we interact with our customers, data, suppliers, our teams, our jobs and the end-to-end operating model of the business we work in - both in terms of the 'what' and the 'how'.

Given the speed in which digital transformation is happening (or must happen to remain competitive and drive a faster return on investment), business cases and product lifecycles are increasingly being shortened. Consequently, organisations are looking at merger and acquisition (M&A) activities to reduce their risk, by acquiring an existing proven capability and customer base and to attain new competences rather than grow their own.

When delivered well, M&As can:

- Provide access to new markets, new customers and, in some cases, access to different countries

- Diversify portfolio with proven products and services, which can be quicker than if organisations self-build

- Be more cost effective than building the capability from scratch

1

- Provide greater market share and influence

- Enable new possibilities, capabilities and creativity thinking

- Give access to a skilled workforce

However, around two thirds of M&As aren't delivered well! You only have to search 'failure rates of M&As' to come across some horrifying statistics, which make you wonder why organisations undertake M&As in the first place.

The ten most common pitfalls of M&A failures are:

1. Insufficient clarity on the customer value proposition (differentiated value as defined by the customer)

2. Inadequate understanding of wider market dynamics, changes to the business environment, or an incomplete assessment of alternative options

3. Lack of a clear medium-to-longer-term strategy defining future benefits beyond the initial M&A integration activity

4. Inability to free up the appropriate level of capable business-as-usual (BAU) resource, ensuring the new operating model is based on true operational reality

5. Cultural assessment and change management issues, with poor employee/customer communication and engagement

6. Integration issues created due to a lack of clarity of execution and integration process issues

7. Unrealistic assessment of the true cost of integration - with direct and associated costs overlooked due to a lack of operational realism

8. Insufficient understanding of the change capacity within an organisation to deliver both the M&A and BAU activities

9. Poor risk management

10. Negotiation and valuation errors

When you read this list of M&A pitfalls, you may question 'how and why do businesses fail on these?' Excluding the commercial financial elements of the deal itself (not covered in this book), M&As can often go wrong due to underestimating the level of emotional response to the change by leaders in both organisations. Any organisational culture change is hard, but in M&A you're multiplying that by two (double the trouble, meaning double the risk), therefore increasing the probability of failure.

Some leaders may still think that when it comes to change - you simply define it, design it and then deploy it. As long as you're clear as a leader on why it makes sense, people should just get on and do it. Neuroscience tells us however, that's not the case. As humans we're all impacted by our emotional response when it comes to change, whether we show it or acknowledge it.

On average our brain scans the environment around us for possible danger or 'threat' situations five times every second.   If our brain sees what it deems to be a 'threat' situation it will enact a 'flight, fight or freeze response' and change at work is deemed for the majority, to be a 'threat' situation.

The perceived level of that change to us as an individual - the certainty of it; our ability to control it; the impact it may have on our status, and whether we deem it to be fair - will ultimately determine how we respond to the change (Meaning whether we move towards it, resist it, reject it or run from it).

How quickly we do that, depends on the level of the change and whether we believe the change benefits or negatively impacts us.

This can mean where change seems logical on paper to a leadership team, it may not seem that way to the person who you're asking to change. (Based on their personal assessment of the perceived threat given their status quo and whether they see it as positive or negative).

As an outcome not all responses from your team will be rational and even if people do see the M&A as positive, the speed to change is unlikely to be quick for those heavily impacted.

In addition, what trips up organisations during M&A activity is their inability to fully understand the depth and duration, or leadership support required from both organisations to deliver the associated change.

For example:

- The support required to articulate clear differentiated value-added benefits to customers and employees on why you're undertaking the M&A

- Understanding how both organisations *really* work

- Managing people through their emotional change curve while you're in the middle of considering your own

All of these aren't easy to do. They're also time consuming and many leaders are asked to do this on top of the day job.

'How to lead through M&A using 20 easy insights' is intended to be a short and sweet read. Read it, drop it in your work bag and check back-in as you go through your M&A. It's been designed to provide learning and insights which I've seen deployed when there's been a level of complex change required. These 'know-hows' have been gained through my experience on leadership, M&As and complex transformational change in large organisations. There may be others, but these are my top 20.

To keep it simple I've broken the book into three sections:

- How M&A pitfalls might show up in an organisation unintentionally. (Let's be honest, people who led failed M&As aren't stupid. They're talented business professionals like you and me, who didn't set out to fail)

- My top know-how insights on how to address the pitfalls

- A summary of how the know-how aligns loosely to the M&A process (I stress *loosely* as leading complex M&A change is not linear, it's more like a rollercoaster), plus a quick insight on 'what good looks like' regarding measures

Dwight D. Eisenhower stated leadership is "the art of getting someone else to do something you want done, because **they** want to do it."

Leading a successful M&A however, adds an extra level of complexity. It's about getting someone else to do something you want done, because they want to do it - while you and they go through a change curve in an environment of uncertainty.

Delivering a successful M&A will require you:

- To demonstrate emotional leadership qualities that compels and captures the hearts and minds of employees and customers - making them believe in the new organisation and getting them to change to the new way of working, despite the uncertainty the M&A will bring

- To operate in your bigger better self and be as clear as you can on the reality in which both organisations operate now and in the future

- Your leadership team and your peers to have the best business plan and clear rationale for why the two organisations should come together

Overview

Overview

The following provides an overview of how the common pitfalls show up (inner white circle); how they translate in to the ten most common business process issues as stated in the introduction (inner grey circle) and how the 'know-how' insight will help address them (outer white circle).

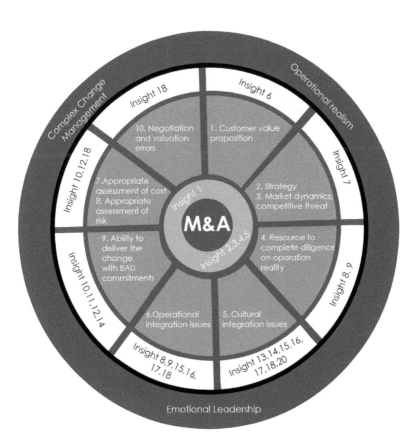

With all complex change, there isn't a silver bullet to fix all. It's unlikely you'll do an activity once, tick the box and move on. You'll need continual leadership, communication and change management capabilities to be successful.

You'll move forward, you'll move back, you'll make mistakes, you'll repeat the same message and reinforce soooooo many times. Some things will make you scream with frustration, others will make you smile or cry with joy, pride or just plain relief!

Being aligned, agile and flexible are the cornerstones of good M&A leadership. Be clear on your destination, why you need to make the journey and accept that your initial plan will change. Most importantly try and have some fun on the way! You'll learn a lot.

Section 1: Pitfall Insights 1-5
Common leadership and operational
pitfalls of an M&A

Pitfall Insight 1. *The sad fact is – a majority of M&As fail*

Reporting on statistics researched by Harvard Business Review[1], Forbes[2] state that 70-90% of M&A activities fail to meet the desired business outcome and objectives. While more recent analysis shows an improvement in the trend (especially for smaller company acquisitions), the sad point is too many M&As are still failing.

Why is this? According to Gartner[3] 44% are due to poorly executed integration activities. In my experience however, it's not the focus on the delivery

---

[1]   The Trade-Offs for Buyers and Sellers in Mergers and Acquisitions. Harvard Business Review Mar 2017
[2]   Forbes: The Three Reasons Why Tech M&A Deals Fail To Deliver Value by Chris Barbin Oct 2017
[3]   HR's Role in Mergers and Acquisitions Gartner 2006

of the commercial finance activities of the M&A (in fact if anything these are over focused on), it's the lack of focus on the wider operational impact of the M&A; defining the ongoing benefits via a medium-term strategy; understanding the costs of integration, and the emotional response to the change.

Insufficient clarity on how both organisations work day-to-day is a common pitfall. Without a true assessment of the similarities and differences, costs and benefits, the timescales to deliver can be distorted in the business case. This can prevent an appropriate assessment of alternative options, which could meet the strategic ambitions or objectives of the business.

Being clear on why an M&A is the right option compared to others, in both the short and medium term, will help provide a 'true north' for leaders when the going gets tough.

M&A is not just about new revenue streams or capabilities, or the cost savings of merging back office functions. Being able to articulate the M&A in terms of the value it brings for your customers and employees, by when and how, now and in the future - is equally as important as the financial and capability synergies the M&A will create.

Pitfall Insight 2. *You get married before you've even dated!*

It's not new news that M&As are often referred to as a marriage, because in essence they are. However, you don't *really* know the organisation you're merging with or acquiring, even if you were previously a customer or a supplier. The relationship will often be different once you're 'living under one roof' and you fully understand how things really work behind closed doors. Before that, it's a bit like being in the honeymoon period after the first few dates!

Think of it like an episode of 'Married at First Sight' – the TV programme where couples are matched by psychologists, vicars and dating experts and meet for the first time on their wedding day. Viewers often see:

- The initial heady excitement of first love at the altar, turn into horror
- They find out the person they married leaves their towel (or worse!) on the floor and they're not really invested in the relationship after all
- This is followed by a swift visit by a relationship expert who matched them in the first place
- It generally ends with one half of the married couple crying on the sofa, stating they made a commitment of marriage and are determined to make it work. Whilst the other half has already salvaged as much as they can from the relationship and TV appearances, is out with their mates down the pub and chalking it up to one of those 'I should have thought about this more' life experiences.

We all know the 'Married at First Sight' concept has an exceptional high risk of failure. Just because you both want to be married and meet all the required facial and height criteria, it doesn't mean you're a good lasting match. Yet weirdly we manage M&As in a similar format!

We leave the majority of the matchmaking to a handful of experts - either external consultants, internal project teams or financial colleagues – who may have limited involvement delivering the benefits post the M&A transaction.

With limited operational hands-on experience, the planning and advisory team may focus more on the tangible elements of the match and make logical assumptions given their level of understanding. They'll be less likely to consider the cost of amalgamating two cultures and the associated cost of the change programme.

To be fair 'change' it's hard to define, hard to grapple with, and for many it's not often a workstream that's considered. It just sits under the People/HR workstream doesn't it?

Post transaction it's full steam ahead to deliver the business benefits, which often become sacrosanct once the deal is signed. Once again this regularly focuses more on tangible benefits, with limited activities in the project plan to develop a combined organisational culture, with supporting 'getting to know you' activities.

Often there is a tick box culture workshop, run as a upsell by the advisory consultants. Post workshop everyone nods at the output and says it was very insightful, yet they do nothing with it because they don't know how to – given culture is often people's perception and it's hard to address. The conclusion is that a few good communications will address it and the responsibility is handed over to the comms team. The hot potato that no one wants to own!

Newly married board executives can also fail to get to grips with differences in 'the way we do things around here' within both organisations. They become frustrated that people in their teams are not moving or changing quickly enough to meet the business benefits, despite telling them on numerous team calls. Leaders who underestimate the power of culture, do so at their peril. Why? because **culture always trumps change**.

Pitfall Insight 3. *When defining the original business case, operational reality of both organisations is often unknown and benefit realisation is overestimated.*

Due to the need for confidentiality during the M&A planning, advisory and transaction, many of the Subject Matter Experts (across all levels of both organisations) are unlikely to be engaged in the initial business benefit assessment. The output from that assessment will therefore not be based on true 'operational reality'. By this we mean the way things are actually done within the business, given the availability of resources (e.g. people, process, systems, finance etc), as opposed to how they are believed to be done either by perception, or how they are documented by operational processes or policies.

As leaders we've all worked on operational efficiency programmes at one point in our careers. We've looked at the spreadsheets, used logic and compared and contrasted one team's performance to another. As experienced leaders we know to take the time to find the cause of why things are the way they are. We do this by asking questions to those performing the tasks, to make sure we're not comparing apples with oranges. However, with M&A activity it's not always possible to ask and realistically you can't sign-up large numbers to a non-disclosure agreement. Therefore, risk is created in the integration plan pre transaction. Post transaction not enough flexibility is added to enable you to go back, change and reforecast.

The common pitfall is a belief that the two organisations are more similar then they really are. You think that bringing the two together will work perfectly.

For example: When you look at a spreadsheet, there can be an automatic assumption that a finance person in company A is the same as the finance person in company B. With a bit of training you'll be able to combine two roles and quickly make one, right?

Not always and often not in the desired timescales of the plan, especially if your project team assessing the benefits of the M&A are not ofay with local employment laws (TUPE, Unions, Works Councils) and don't give adequate consideration to knowledge transfer etc.

M&A business case owners can underestimate the complexity, resource availability and the time it will take before they can cash the cheque on the savings. This is particularly true if there are other strategic transformations going on in either organisation, which require the same resources and change capacity.

Consequently, risk management is often underplayed, as no one wants to be the nay-sayer on the deal team. Deal teams can often become so blinded by the relationship with the other organisation, the M&A itself and the need to bring-in the capability, they can't see the true operational reality, associated cost and heavy lifting required to make two organisations become one.

Pitfall Insight 4. *M&A activities trigger a flight, fight or freeze response from employees and customers who may leave you.*

Put very simply, our brains have been programmed to manage a flight, fight or freeze response since the dawn of time - although in today's business world, we don't all go to work to fight Sabre Tooth Tigers (although it may feel like it sometimes!). As leaders we deal with the modern environmental factors that can create stressful situations and trigger a flight, fight or freeze response.

M&A activities generate uncertainty for an organisation, its employees and its customers. M&As in the main mean change. Organisational change generates worry about job losses, changes in manager and/or location and the way people work.

People are naturally programmed to move away from a state of threat or stress (such as job uncertainty) and move towards one of certainty. With on average 30% of employees deemed redundant after an M&A in the same industry,[4] people are aware of the potential risk of job losses. This can create an issue regarding the retention of talent and those with a desirable skill set who, if not managed, will seek new roles elsewhere.

At the other end of the scale, unmotivated employees may take their 'foot off the gas' as they withdraw from the uncertainty or go into freeze mode. As an output you may see productivity levels drop, as well as an increase in both sick absence and mental health absence.

From a customer and supplier perspective, there's uncertainty regarding areas like quality, brand identity, product assurance, consistency of staff contacts and product delivery during the M&A alignment. If 70-90% of M&A fail, a perception of uncertainty across the ecosystem will be common and is a real threat to business continuity.

Competitors may also use this opportunity to poach not only your staff, but your customers too. They can use the time, when they perceive you to be focused on delivering internal acquisition milestones, to dial-up any uncertainty regarding your ability to supply and on your stability as an organisation. This of course becomes a lot easier for them if they have just recruited your sales and service staff (due to a perceived lack of job security during the M&A).

[4]   Surviving M&A by Mitchell Lee Marks, Philip Mirvis, Ron Ashkenas. Harvard Business Review. April 2017

Pitfall Insight 5. *M&A survivor syndrome can bring out the worst in leaders.*

Flight, fight or freeze responses are within everyone. Too often organisations overlook support for the people leading the change e.g. the Board, the Senior Leadership Team and the Subject Matter Experts. By default they are informed first, then expected to communicate the change and support others without having had the time to come to terms and accept the change for themselves.

With an amalgamation of two organisations it's more than likely there will be fewer senior roles. Senior leaders are usually wedded to the boundaries of their roles, having aspired and proven their worth and in some instances, even fought and negotiated to get there.

Fear of loss of personal value and identity for leaders will have an impact on their emotional state. Who we work for, our teams, our job title and the value we bring, provides us with a sense of purpose, identity and a level of control. M&As by their nature challenge this. They challenge the status quo of our job and by default us as a leader. Consequently, leaders can feel uncertainty due to a foreboding sense of loss, relatedness, fairness and ultimately status for which they cannot control. However, given their capability of resilience, they often won't raise their concerns directly. Instead, they will try and to manage or manipulate control.

When not managed, negative behaviours associated with flight, fight or freeze can become more serious as leaders go through survival syndrome (e.g. scapegoating, land grabbing and disengagement). Due to a leader's visibility and influence, the toxicity of their behaviour can start to flow down into the organisation.   This can change the employee and customer perception of the leaders themselves and the M&A. Going from one of positivity to negativity.

Fight behaviours can also be witnessed as Executives start jostling for position. They start raising their profiles, being more openly proactive with stakeholder management or claiming ownership of critical business priorities to make themselves indispensable or to maintain their level of status.

On the other hand, for the less resilient (or less invested), you may see individuals go in to a 'freeze' state. This is in terms of their cognitive ability (i.e. 'it's too much for me to think about right now'). They may withdraw from wider interaction and debate on the M&A, withholding open and honest critique and focusing inwards on their local priorities. Leaders will lean towards others with a similar outlook and this can create a 'them and us' mentality which will easily be picked up by the wider organisation.

For those considering 'flight', where commercially viable they will seek and line up external employment opportunities, working out the most opportune and lucrative moment to leave. The outcome could mean you have leadership gaps at a critical moment and a loss of talent.

Where communication is not managed well, this can increase uncertainty of job security in lower levels of the organisation. It can also increase the level of 'threat' created by the M&A and thoughts of 'what does this mean for me?'

Leaders and the shadow they cast, are instrumental in the success of the M&A. In times of uncertainty a leader's perception become the gospel truth within an organisation. The alignment of the leadership team within an M&A is critical in settling the two organisations, aligning the cultures and delivering the benefits on time. A misaligned leadership team who don't sing from the same hymn sheet is a recipe for disaster, creates delays and toxicity within the programme and the wider business-as-usual organisation.

Know-How Insights 6-18
Emotional Leadership and
operational realism

Know-How Insight 6. *Be clear on the value the M&A will deliver for all stakeholders especially your customers.*

M&A activity clearly creates disruption. If you're going to upset the status quo, you need to be really clear on why. Where is it taking you from and to? Why is doing the M&A better than doing nothing? In a nutshell, what are the undisputed benefits and what is the strategy!

Sometimes the need to improve operating costs, asset return and acquiring new capabilities can overwhelm the rationale and the wider benefits of the M&A. It's a bit like being focused on having a baby to save a marriage, rather than considering marriage counselling or a date night first! If you can't articulate the 'why' 'how' and the 'what' in terms of realistic value, benefits and unique market differentiators, you're likely to find yourself part of the 70-90% M&A failure statistic.

From day one it's important to be able to articulate true customer value, from what customers perceive is value. Does it give customers something they can't already get in the market and is it of true differentiated value? Acquiring attributes that are too similar to your own often means customers can buy either/or from you (portfolio cannibalisation), and that can be one of the fastest ways to erode value from the deal.

This may seem obvious, but so many times it's overlooked. It's not tested from a customer perspective prior to the M&A deal and means the outcome of forecasted growth is not achieved.

As part of the M&A Strategy, Planning and Advisory phase you need to ensure you can define and articulate simply why the M&A is taking place, in terms of:

- Why it's good for your customers and shareholders. Can the M&A drive real value from a customer perspective against the competition? If so for how long? This needs to be something that the competition can't replicate in the time it takes you to complete the M&A. Otherwise by default it's no longer a unique point of differentiation

- Why is it good for your employees? How is the work going to be done when the two organisations come together and by whom?

- Why is it good for the bottom line now and in the future?

- How far should the merger go without eroding value from either organisation?

If you can't clearly articulate a sustained differentiator or pivot point in the market - that will create value from a customer perspective more than any other option - think twice before starting the M&A journey!

Know-How Insight 7. *Be clear on the medium and long-term strategy.*

In a medium to large organisation it will take at least 18 months to deliver fully embedded and sustained organisational change. So defining a clear strategy and associated purpose that both organisations can relate to is critical. It goes without saying, if it's a strategy it needs to articulate value for the next 3-5 years, supported by the financial forecast and executable plan. You don't want one of those fancy PowerPoint strategies that's communicated once, delivers nothing and sits in a draw.

If your strategy can articulate and define the value of the M&A from your customers and market perspective, then the articulation for your wider stakeholder community (e.g. financiers, shareholders and most importantly employees) is so much easier. You want the outcome to be that the reader, whoever they are, clearly understands the reasons why you're bringing the two organisations together and can see and feel that the future is rosier and more successful as a combined organisation.

Articulating the value for all stakeholders is critical both now and throughout the integration. Show how future deliverables build towards your strategy and plan and don't skimp on leadership communications. Ensure that initially it's seen as a shared responsibility, with proactive participation from both organisations and that both organisations are aligned behind it.

Areas your strategy should address should include:

- The combined vision and purpose for the new organisation

- Why the M&A will provide market differentiation based on customer needs

- Clear articulation of the immediate, medium, and long-term benefits

- 'What's in it for me' statements for all stakeholder groups both internally and externally

- A high-level timeline of what you're going to do, when and why

- The support that's required to be successful from the organisation and its employees, mitigating any known risks/concerns

- Provides the high-level steps on how the organisation is going to get there

Don't underestimate the power of an organisation's purpose. It's different to your strategy. It identifies the core reason why your organisation came together to exist and why you will do what you do as a combined entity. When bringing two organisations together, the ability to quickly articulate a combined, easy to remember purpose that people can identify with, will help address and reduce anxiety for your employees and customers.

Support the launch with strong communications which state why the elected dual organisation combined team came up with the new purpose. What it means for them and your customers (Vox Pops - short video montages - can be effective here). Creating a team of change agents, across both companies, can help the wider organisation associate and resonate with the new purpose quicker than if it just comes from senior management. Customer confirmation will also provide assurance on the market need.

In addition, employees seeing peers being given opportunities to determine the future will reduce anxiety of being 'done to' and provide a feeling of increased control. Signpost early how people can get involved. Follow up locally with further discussion about the strategy and purpose and include an appropriate feedback loop.

Building relatedness, motivation and gaining 'buy-in' to your strategy will be crucial. And remember, if you want to enable the art of 'getting someone else to do something you want done, because they want to do it' (Dwight D. Eisenhower), you'll need to listen, act and communicate. Ideally co-create as much as possible with a dual organisation teams and focus groups, represented by all levels of the organisation.

Know-How Insight 8. *Date as much as possible before you marry.*

Let's be honest when the deal is signed there will be pressure from multiple areas to show progress and to get the ball rolling so you can cash the cheque.

Around 60% of the work effort in a successful M&A is in the alignment of tangible deliverables such as customer accounts, processes, systems, assets etc. The remaining 40% should address the 'softer' functional elements like culture and values to embed and sustain the change. Given the latter is something that's not normally written down, it's more 'the way it's done round here' you'll need time to understand exactly what this is to ensure change can be executed.

Nine times out of ten if the change you propose is contrary to organisational culture, culture will trump the change. In these situations, to execute change successfully you either need to change the culture first or amend the proposed change to align with the cultural norm.

Given culture change is hard to measure and define, many organisations think about it and then simply ignore it. However, knowing if the change is contrary to an organisation's belief system, in terms of what employees deem as fair, relatable and socially acceptable, will help you understand if people will adopt the change or disregard it.

One of the best ways to understand culture is undertaking what the Americans call a 'prisoner exchange' (who said romance was dead?). This will help you get a feel of the similarities and differences between the two companies. To do this, pick a few trusted and open people from all grades and areas within both organisations. Get them to swap roles and then 'walk in each other's shoes'. This way you get to dispel the myths and perceptions and get a true understanding of what it's really like on the hard and soft elements. Ensure that the feedback and findings can be given in a candid and structured way and don't limit your 'prisoner exchange' to just HR colleagues (as they're seen as being accountable for culture). Pick all functions across the organisations.

Where possible build this activity into your business case timeframes. Review M&A workstreams and associated benefits once the Prisoner Exchange and feedback is complete, and then adjust the deliverables/benefits based on the findings.

Revalue the size and likelihood of any risk and how it impacts any previous versions of your business case.

How you get to the outcome is better than not getting there at all. With M&As, being open to change and variation to the original business case and plan is important. As we've said previously, on day one nobody truly understands the detail of both organisations well enough to have a definitive business case. As leadership rule of thumb, be clear on 'what' you want to do, 'how' people get there is something you may want to be a bit more flexible on.

Know-How Insight 9. *Deliver the 'best of both'*
learning from each other.

Most organisations have similar processes,
however how they operate within those processes
differ. Assessing activities and processes in both
organisations is a good way to understand the
similarities and differences, as well as understanding
who does what best.

Whether you call it a Blueprint, an activity-based org
chart, an operating model or a process taxonomy -
reviewing and comparing what both organisations
do and how they do it, is one of the best and quickest
way to assess the level of alignment and integration
needed. It also helps you understand the associated
risks between organisations in the short, medium and
long term.

Based on your strategy and unique differentiation
points, firstly define the desired customer experience
you want to deliver with available resources. Then
align your operating model, costs and resources
behind it. Get this right and it should set you up for
optimum success.

Ask functional Subject Matter Experts from both
organisations to walk through their own core
functional processes that support the end-to-end
operating model. A sales core process operating
model is provided as an example.

Example of a sales core process operating model model.

Customer Sales Strategy	Segmentation and growth plan	Portfolio alignment and development
	Channel management	Channel partners and alliances

Sales Operations and Management	Organisational design	Resource allocation management
	Target setting and KPIs	Performance and sales management
	Value proposition / campaigns	

Sales Processes and Execution	Account planning	Account management
	Opportunity management	Forecasting
	End to end sales process	

Sales Tools, Technology, Data and Insight	Systems and Tools	Data architecture
	Insight and Reporting	AI and Security

Sales People and Capability	Remuneration, incentives, pay plan and reward	Competency and capability development
	Sales culture, leadership and mindset	

Ask the team to consider:

- Do both organisations have these process/ capabilities and if not should they? If the answer is yes, will the existing process/capabilities work for both?

- Where both organisations execute the same process, look to provide a RAG (Red, Amber, Green) status in terms of how closely they're aligned. Out of the two, is there a more optimal approach?

- Is that optimal approach the best? Does it take the best of both organisations? Is it fit for purpose? Is it the best in the market and/or the industry? Does it deliver the best customer experience? Would your customers rate it as 'the best'?

- Where there is no 'best' - given the resources you have, the priority of that specific process against the strategy of the organisation and the change capacity - what's the opportunity to enhance the process for both organisations? What is external leading practice?

- If it's an area of differentiation as defined in the strategy, can it/should it be optimised further to provide a greater return?

- Could both organisations adopt the best of both? Are there mitigating factors that need to be removed or managed before this can happen, based on operational reality and your combined risk register?

- Define and design your plan of activity

If you've made a conscious decision however, not to take any action to align and integrate processes/capabilities - are you clear about the business cost/customer and organisational impact of doing nothing?

The critical part to getting the output right and optimising the 'best of both' is the mind-set of the individuals doing the review. You want to avoid game playing (whereby people try to hold on to their own ways of working), empire building (in order to protect their status quo), and a resilience to change (which ends in stalemate leading to a form of bartering or zero progress).

You're looking for the reviewers to be:

- Detached from the current status. Be unbiased in terms of who does what, why or how they do it, yet deeply engaged in making the M&A work and making the combined organisations better as a whole

- Able to the see what the market and customer experience will look like for the new M&A. What ideally the organisation should look like to support that experience, based on the M&A strategy and goals

- Capable of articulating how customers will interact with the new organisation, in terms of how they will buy, be served, billed and supported etc. This will enable them to define the aligned operating processes and the linkages, dependencies and risks within it

- Able to apply operational realism. Creating solutions within the culture and resources available. Prioritising opportunities which provide paradoxical benefits e.g. improving customer satisfaction whilst reducing operational costs through improved automation.

Add a small percentage of disgruntled employees into the review process as they provide clear insight into the things that don't work. By involving them, they feel included and more in control of the change. If you able to convert them from a 'moaner' to an 'owner' of the solution, this can have a positive impact on the wider organisation. If known negative people are positive about the M&A, then others are more likely to feel it's got to be a good thing.

Remember: Choosing who and setting up the context on how you want people to complete the review in terms of mindset and outlook, can be just as important as the review itself in terms of outcome.

Know–How Insight 10. *Don't skimp to make the business case work.*

Being realistic on your operating integration costs and timescales is key. M&A managers can fall in love with the opportunity of an M&A, then start tweaking the cost and benefits to make sure it takes place, just because they're wedded to the idea. Stepping back and being pragmatic to the wider costs and tasks, both in the short and longer term is important. M&As are too big a commitment to just mitigate this year's goals.

Don't be tempted, in order to get the business case to fly, to exclude any wider associated operational budget requests or costs. Sometimes delaying investment just means you rack up a bigger bill down the line, you don't mitigate your risks properly and you deliver a poor customer experience as a consequence. As with all business cases, getting the balance right so the opportunity flies without trying to solve all organisational woes is fundamental. That's why having an in-scope and out-scope agreement is key, so you can be clear on what needs to be done and what makes good business sense if resource is available.

Also be clear on what's a true cost associated with the M&A and what's an associated cost of incremental activities you'll deliver as part of the M&A (that will either save costs later or drive known organisational benefits earlier).

Document risks at every stage from deal planning into transaction, as well as integration and transformation stages. Even document issues that can be resolved quickly once you are able to engage with operational teams. From a psychological perspective if you involve people by asking for their input to a problem or on how things could work better going forward, you'll help to reduce their stress created by uncertainty through engagement.

Don't just look at risk from the perspective of the M&A project. Review other activities, projects and programmes that are going on in both organisations. Do these become less of a priority due to the M&A or should they be put on hold, aligned, prioritised or ceased? Look to combine programmes to reduce or realign costs and resources and strengthen benefits within established programmes.

It's also a great opportunity to cluster analyse your risks from both the M&A and your legacy operations. You can sometimes generate solutions that mitigates the M&A risks while delivering a business as usual benefit. And if you can remove organisational annoyances for the customer at the same time as the M&A, it helps to reinforce the M&A as a 'good thing' as well as helping to reduce ongoing operational costs.

For example: migrating to a single customer database as part of the M&A integration is not going to get cheaper with time (given time means you'll have more records to migrate). Yet the cost of a data cleanse is probably something the business would need to do/or should have done irrespective of the M&A. It therefore may make sense to do the data cleanse at the time you merge the databases.

Lastly challenge your thinking - should you and could you be doing more?

If you're going to change, what is the best outcome given the priorities and resources available and the associated risk? M&As are risky and many organisations just want to deliver the activity as quickly as possible, however I challenge that thinking given we're now in a world of digital disruption.

Taking time and calculated risks to really transition and transform should improve the customer experience, provide competitive advantage, improve employee satisfaction and reduce overall operating and change implementation costs. Where opportune and considered I would say take the opportunity to do this. Think wider to optimise the return on investment, changing once not twice within your resource budget. In addition to the benefits above, it removes continual uncertainty, change fatigue in the organisation and delivers benefits faster.

You do however, need to be on-point with your risk and change capability assessment to get it right.

For example: When reviewing the combined portfolio opportunity and customer data as part of the M&A front office alignment activity, you could also consider including an additional open source data feed. This could give you a more informed and a broader view of the customer to help support segmentation, opportunities, targets and forecasts etc. In addition, you could also include an Artificial Intelligence platform to provide an enhanced Data Analytics capability in the new organisation. If you are changing your systems, processes and training as part of the M&A, adding enhanced functionality maybe an opportunity.

Know-How Insight 11. *Be clear on your capacity to execute and deliver the change.*

Don't underestimate the change capacity of an organisation. They all have a ceiling point.

Think about organisational change as a bucket. You want to fill the bucket to the right level to optimise the carrying capacity. If you overfill it the contents overflow and you lose the excess, or worst-case scenario the bucket breaks and all the content washes away. Change capacity in an organisation is similar. Do too much and the benefits are never fully realised. It creates too much stress and uncertainty for employees to align behind all the change required of them. To regain control they'll just continue with what's familiar, ignore the change and do as little as possible. You may also see an increase in absenteeism, productivity reduction and Union/Works Council involvement, as employees ask for support to maintain the status quo and remove or reduce the level of 'threat'.

Successful change relies on the following three things, in addition to the change itself being fit for purpose and aligned to culture:

- The first is 'hard resources' like people, budgets etc to support the change for the duration that it will take to embed and sustain it into BAU.

  ° In most cases insufficient resource is allocated to execute and sustain the change. This can lead to business benefits not being realised, or at worst a migration back to old working practices, as key stakeholders move away from the programme too soon before full adoption

  ° Good change practice means allocating 40% of any project budget to the implementation activity (training, associated operational shrinkage, communication programmes etc)

  ° Don't underestimate the time it will take to truly embed and sustain change. As a rule of thumb assume 18 months for a medium to large organisation.

- The second is the organisation's culture and leadership capability to sponsor, coach and support people through the change.

- Thirdly, and often forgotten, consequence management for not changing. Neuroscience tells us that people are five times more likely to move away from a negative situation than move towards a positive one.

During change you will move through a standard distribution curve of migration and adoption. 20% will be trailblazers and will move and adopt the change first. You need to showcase the benefits this group is receiving to encourage and move the 60% mass majority. You then have the 20% laggard population that will remain aligned to the old ways. If you're not clear to the laggards what the consequences will be for not moving (i.e. rationale for the M&A), they'll remain unchanged as they don't perceive any benefit in moving. Where this behaviour continues, you risk the lower end of your mass majority falling back into old ways of working if they believe it to be easier. Over time if the laggard population is never addressed it will grow, as people will perceive that change is a choice. When this becomes part of your organisational culture due to lack of consequence, the cost and timescales to deploy further change will increase.

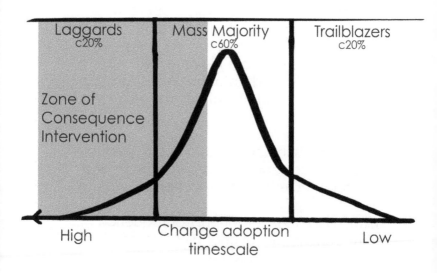

Depending on the size, complexity, depth of the M&A, available resource, the change capacity and risk etc, it's unlikely you'll be able to move to the desired end state of the change in one go. You may need to move the organisation to a mid-point transition state first. If this is the case, be clear on this up front in both your plan and in your communications to your employees.

A transition state can help you build in a 'Prisoner Exchange' programme (refer to Know-How Insight 8). It also gives you time to align your systems and systems architecture, gain buy-in, migrate resource to the M&A programme from BAU and align a wider programme of activities. The downside is it can lengthen the transformation and the period of uncertainty. Sometimes organisations feel a transition state may not be an option, especially if the M&A was undertaken to acquire a first-mover advantage in the market. If this is the case, speed to execute might be a paramount objective.

Here's a cautionary word: A swan can often be seen swimming calmly to the external world, while all the time it's paddling furiously under the water. A motivated team who see the benefits of a transition period to get the job done right, will often hide the transition cracks from their customers - enabling you to move to market quickly. If you have a motivated team, who are engaged and invested in the outcome, they're often better than a compliant team who just get the job done because they're told. High-performing, engaged teams who have a purpose they believe in, are amazing at being swans - as long as the change isn't indefinite, and you keep channels of communication open.

Know–How Insight 12. *Define upfront what can't be broken or disrupted as you complete the M&A.*

Knowing what an M&A can't disrupt within the customer experience and within the organisation should be considered upfront and mitigated against. It's important to ring-fence the initial work to ensure business as usual can continue and to plan how the integration will happen, along with the timings and impact of each project rollout.

You want to integrate as quickly as possible to give more certainty to your customers and employees, but you don't want your business put at risk or people to feel overwhelmed by the change. Putting appropriate measures in place to track any disruption while the change is going through, gives you early indicators and will help to mitigate and remove risk as you merge. It will also help gauge the amount of change your customers and employees can absorb. Areas that can't be broken or disrupted should be easy to identify through your strategy. Picking these

areas to track and monitor pre, during and post the M&A is a sound investment.

For example: Many organisations want to avoid any disruption to their customer experience. Taking the current customer experience journeys in both organisations and tracking critical moments of truth on a single automated system with enhanced analytics, will help you remove the risk of your M&A activities impacting the customer.

Another associated benefit of being clear about what can't be broken or disrupted, is that it will help you decipher the appropriate resource split on BAU verses the M&A and the appropriate allocation based on risk. Too often you'll see that failed M&As didn't free up critical BAU resource to support the design of the new operating model.

Asking some of these simple questions up front, can mean critical organisational values can be managed proactively during the M&A and be safe guarded in a cost-effective manner, rather than reactively when things have gone wrong.

Know-How Insight 13. *The Leadership team will need support to be their bigger selves.*

Pitfall insight five covered some of the behaviours that may show up as leaders start to assume or understand what the M&A might mean for them. What's often overlooked though is the program of change management for leaders themselves i.e. the Board, Managing Directors, Senior Executives who support everyone else. This has two potential impacts:

1. If you have a Board where toxic relationships already exist, there is the potential to increase the levels of toxicity in times of uncertainty

2. If the senior team are not united behind the M&A due to their own uncertainty and concerns, they are likely to leak this into the wider organisation, consciously or unconsciously. Thereby making communications from the senior team misaligned and creating greater uncertainty for the wider organisation

Senior leaders are pivotal in making an M&A work. How they handle themselves and the shadows they cast, can either alleviate fear for stakeholders or elevate it. A small investment in senior executive coaching to support and accelerate them through their own change curve is a sound investment. Surveys by Salesforce[5] estimate generally a 17% performance enhancement between those coached and those not.

It will also help get new executive relationships off to a good start between the two organisations, as well as uplifting general leadership capability. It will alleviate some stress from the CEO, M&A project leads and Chief Operating Officers, by providing an extra pair of hands and ears.

Executive assessment to support the CEO and COO is another activity to provide an impartial view of leadership capability (in terms of who is best to remain in the newly combined organisation), given relationships at this level are often deep and dependent.

[5]   'What is the ROI for sales coaching'. 2013 Blog by Kevin Micalizzi. www.salesforce.com.

Know–How Insight 14. *Accept there will be some headcount reductions, but ensure you retain your talent.*

In nine out of ten M&As, there will be operating cost savings to be made. Often this means losing c30% of staff from all levels of the organisation.

Attention to talent retention at all levels is of parallel importance. Early identification of both talent and critical resources in both organisations is critical. Be clear what your retention programmes need to be in order to be attractive and then execute to mitigate risk.

Most M&As deliver some form of restructure. You need to keep it as contained as possible until you're ready to communicate, then pull the plaster off as quick as you can. Long extended restructures help no one - not your employees, not your customers and certainly not your business. Providing purpose, understanding, clarity and certainty as quickly as you can is key. Moving to a transitional Organisational Design is better than ongoing communications that state 'change is coming', with continually slipping timescales.

Know–How Insight 15. *Communicate, communicate, communicate!*

Understanding your stakeholder groups, their needs and wants and underpinning those with clear internal and external messages and a sustained communications plan is critical. As with any change programme, you need to provide as much certainty and clarity as you can, as quickly as you can.

Most of your communications, in terms of the rationale of the M&A, purpose, strategy and business priorities will need to come from your senior leadership team, so everyone has the same level of understanding on the direction and commitments of the new organisation. Refer to them as you hit key milestones and as you celebrate and recognise success.

Make sure your internal and external messaging are aligned. Having a central key message palette, Q&A and presentation material available for leaders, who can make it relevant for their people, customers and suppliers - will help to provide clarity and importantly consistency. These will need to be updated throughout the lifecycle of the M&A.

When it comes to communications though, one size doesn't fit all, and you'll need to ensure relatedness and relevance in your local messaging e.g. what your finance organisation needs to know from an operational point of view will be different to your marketing department. Leaders should take the core material and add relevant messaging on what it means for their specific function or target group.

Not all communications have to be formal and often having a key few notable evangelists at all levels within the organisation, particularly in core impacted groups, is a good way to build trust and provide an informal feedback loop. Using your people from your 'best of both' analysis (see Know-How Insight 9) can also provide background information and rationale as to why decisions were made.

Key things to consider internally:

- Ensure your top team have the same understanding of the change and agree with the key messages (Your employees talk to each other and compare what they're being told). If you have a top team member off message it creates unnecessary harm and puts the change at risk

- If you are to be successful, your sponsors and change agents need to have a consistently clear definition of the 'as-is' state today for each organisation and why the 'to-be' future state as a combined entity will be better for both

- You'll need to create a regular heartbeat of communication throughout the entire M&A process. This means you'll need a communications plan for the duration of the change (at least 18 months) and you'll need to bolster that with messaging specific to the area/function you're responsible for. Be as open and honest as you can

- Be aware that myths will be created in both organisations, as a leader you need to bust these as quickly as possible, so they don't derail the change

- Always respond to inaccurate or speculative external press activity so your employees understand what's real and consider providing your sales and service staff with a statement they can give to customers if needed

- Create internal feedback/Q&A mechanisms. This will help you listen to the concerns of your employees. Respond quickly and authentically. You'll have tons of questions you won't have the answer for because the change will be work-in-progress. It's ok for you to say that, but you must log and answer them as soon as you can. And if you give employees a timeline of when you will communicate, you must always honour that promise - otherwise why would they believe a word you say?

- Remember people go through the change curve at different rates. You'll need to be patient and be prepared to constantly repeat key messages. When you come to communicate, remember how you felt when first told about the M&A and the questions you had at the start of the process. Put yourself in the shoes of your team for a minute

Key things to consider externally:

- Communicate in a timely manner with all stakeholders. Don't leave it to the press or your competitors to do it for you

- Competitors are likely to communicate with your customers during the M&A process. You'll need to increase your customer conversations or formal communications, in order to alleviate customer concerns and excite them about the capabilities and opportunities of the new organisation

- Assess any or inaccurate press speculation and communicate directly with customers, shareholders and suppliers if you need to

- Communicate new deliverables and benefits from the M&A when they are fit to go to market. Try and deliver some quick wins as soon as possible and share the good news from a customer perspective.

Know–How Insight 16. *Resistance to change is inevitable. Sometimes it's not rational, but you need to surface it and deal with it to be successful.*

Why is communication so important in an M&A? Because you need to understand the resistance to change and be able to acknowledge it, address it and deal with it as quickly as possible.

Resistance occurs for many reasons e.g. change fatigue, poor sponsorship, organisational stress, cultural alignment, a lack of involvement, or a belief that change isn't happening for the right reason.

If your communications are just one way then it becomes you, the leader or leadership team who own the change. People will simply do it because they must, not because they want to and they end up being compliant, rather than owning the change. This isn't ideal as it means you'll often end up using a 'stick approach' to move the majority. This comes with higher costs, both in terms of the investment in leadership time and the time it takes to implement. In addition, it gives you an increased likelihood of failure - not only for the M&A, but subsequent changes as well.

To overcome this, you need trusted sponsors, gold users and great change agents. You'll need a plan and a bunch of experienced people that employees trust, from both organisations, to help you deliver it. They need to get out into the organisation to walk the walk and talk the talk. And they need to reach all impacted levels of the organisation to try and surface resistance and to gain buy-in and involvement.

They need to:

- Be visible

- Be trusted

- Listen to and value the feedback being given

- Reinforce desired behaviours

- Encourage people to discuss their resistance to change in a safe way

- Challenge and flag other non-believers

- Recognise and celebrate progress - however big or small

Mental wellbeing is now thankfully becoming a topic of conversation in business today. People are more willing to share how they felt when they heard about the M&A and what they did to manage themselves through the change curve. Being open about their uncertainty and anxiety via Vox Pops and other channels, helps others though their change curve in a healthier way. It's also good, where you have access to employee counselling services, to give reference to this as well. Remember, some employees may have change in their personal life as well as the M&A. Being considerate to this and providing managers with the appropriate professional support if required is important.

Town Halls are also a great medium to get people together and to talk openly about the change. They can be led by people at all levels within the organisation. If they're setup correctly, they can be a great way of surfacing resistance. They are in no way an ego trip for the presenter. If everyone attending is just nodding and telling you you're wonderful, you've missed the opportunity to understand resistance.

The first few can be demanding as people go through the denial, doubt and uncertainty phase of their change curve, but here are some pointers on how to get them right:

- Actively listen to what's being said and try and meet people face to face. Feedback can be more constructive and genuine when you're sat in front of someone rather than through email or on the phone

- Remember people may be angry. It's a natural emotional response when people feel they've lost control. Always acknowledge someone's values and emotions, because how they feel is important to them. However, it's not acceptable for people to be disrespectful or rude to others, so set some 'behavioural rules' at the start of the meeting that state what you expect

- Never try and out argue someone with logic. What is logical to you, may not be to them. You will just make them more frustrated and more resistance. Keep calm and state the outcome you want to achieve. If they're still unsure how the steps being taken will meet the desired outcome, ask them why they don't align to your point of view and to share their opinion

- Don't be tempted to bargain or barter. Be clear about what needs to be done and why. Bargaining or bartering on the 'what' makes you look weak, moves you off track, dilutes your deliverables and looks like you weren't clear on what you needed to do in the first place

- Confirm your support to the programme and that of the wider local team

- Ensure you remain on message and be clear on where you are today, where you need to get to and why, and how you intend to get there. People might not like what's being done, but if they can understand why and the benefits it will bring, they'll eventually accept it

- Provide clear expectations of what you require from people during the change

- Show you understand people's uncertainty. Ask as many open-ended questions as possible to encourage two-way communication and debate

- Test options and ask for feedback on areas where you need support or new ways of thinking. However, don't ask if you already have the answer as this devalues their opinion and status

- If you want people to get involved in the change, be clear how they can do this and when

- It's ok not to have an answer to a question, but you do need to go back and respond when you do

- You need to stick to your timescales. If you can't meet them, provide an update with a reason why

- Acknowledge the progress made, thank and recognise people both on the M&A team and in the wider business and be honest when things have not gone well too

- Reinforce new behaviours at every opportunity

- Always send a follow-up thank to people for attending, include a synopsis of what you took away and confirm next steps

Repeat Town Halls regularly to demonstrate commitment and progress. You should be able to gauge, by the type and quantity of questions, if you're gaining people's hearts and minds.

Other tools that work well are broadcasted interviews with an interactive Q&A, focus groups, team huddles, brown bag lunches and back to the floor sessions. Remember the more you involve people, the more they'll feel like they're gaining back control. This will help to reduce stress and resistance. It will bring operational realism to your solution and importantly build a commitment to deliver.

Know–How Insight 17. *It's ok to acquire an organisation and not merge into BAU.*

Many organisations, especially in the IT space, are acquiring smaller start-ups to bring new capabilities to their brand. They do this because it often reduces the time and cost of product development and it provides a proven capability as well as an existing customer base.

Often when companies are in their infancy, they're not stifled by bureaucracy and process. This gives them the opportunity to be more creative and be fleet of foot. Industry acquisitions often struggle in these instances to get the right balance between offering parental support and suffocating the acquired child. Too many times the parent company become overzealous with sweating the asset and providing support - thinking they know best. They integrate the acquired business too far, sucking out what was good, creative and dynamic about the business they just bought.

Many people who choose to work for start-ups, identify strongly with creating something from scratch. They like the adaptability, agility and 'build as you go' customer processes and culture.

Sometimes it can be the weirdest and smallest things that trip-up an integration. For example: moving the acquired company to centralised provisioning systems sounds sensible to manage costs. However, if the acquired company are used to simply asking their manager for a new mobile phone and now, they need three sign-off levels and fill in a form via a central provisioning portal, it no longer feels like they're working for a small company. These types of things soon become irritants to employees and if you have a sought-after skilled workforce, your staff could soon be off to join the next growing start-up.

Instances where I've seen acquisitions work well, is where they're moved into a venture business unit within the parent company. Here the acquired child organisation sits as a small business alongside other acquisitions. Support functions and resources may be shared across the ventures at a more senior advisory level. The business ventures are quite autonomous. They maintain their creativity and agility, resources and identity, but utilise some of the benefits and support systems of the parent company.

As the acquired start-up grows, operational support requirements increase, and the culture and ways of working becomes more aligned with the parent organisation. The level of integration can be reviewed as appropriate and this can be one way where you can truly get the best of both.

Know–How Insight 18. *Last but not least…the entrepreneur can be a tricky customer.*

Acquiring a company when the founder of that company in still in situ may need a little more sensitive leadership. That's not to say all are problematic, but let's put it this way - you're buying someone's baby! The baby they conceived; the baby they nurtured; the baby they watched grow and gave up their weekends for, and the baby that's been their life for however many years. With this in mind, you should always ask and be clear on why the entrepreneur is happy to sell:

- If they simply want out or cash in, ensure you complete enough due diligence on the valuation of the company you are going to acquire. It's not that they're being dishonest, but no one is going to call their baby ugly and estimate on the lower end of the company's value. If you don't spend enough time on this, you could find that the valuation gap or the organisation is bigger than you expected

- If they're selling because they want the help and support of a parent company, they could have a skewed view that the parent company has more available assets and deeper pockets than they're willing to give. The risk being a misalignment of the M&A priority. The acquisition of their organisation is often and understandably the number one priority for the entrepreneur. However, it may not be yours

- It's not unusual for entrepreneurs to create their baby because they preferred working for themselves rather than someone else. Many entrepreneurship and business start-ups don't grow beyond a small business size. This in the main (outside of finances), is due to the founder's capability to mitigate risk through appropriate policy and processes and to ensure consistency and growth.   However, it can also be down to the founder's capability to relinquish control via delegation, management and leadership. The later can cause issues with the M&A

With M&As you're not only impacting the founder's status (from the boss to an employee), you're reducing their relatedness from 'owning' to 'sharing'. You think this would be obvious to the entrepreneur but in some instances, they can be blind to it. Their ego gets flattered by the M&A pay cheque and adrenaline of the deal. They often don't fully appreciate their emotional relationship and attachment to their own business, what they're giving up, and what it will mean to work for someone else after all these years.

If the founding owner is going to remain:

- Draw up a working contract based on how you're going to work post the M&A transaction i.e. the roles, responsibilities, accountabilities, mitigations and consequences and the areas they have authority to work autonomously on

- Consider scenarios and mitigations upfront on how you're going to work together and on what. This may start as a conversation over coffee, but you need to document it. You may never need to refer to it, but in times of dispute, performance issues or when emotions are running high, you will be pleased you took the time to agree it up front

- Support the entrepreneur through their change curve, especially if the founder is a key to the asset you have acquired. Hiring a leadership coach as an independent third party can really pay dividends.

Success Insights 19 - 20
Understanding what success looks like

Success Insight 19. *How do you know when you've been successful?*

You'll know when you've been successful when you see, hear and feel the organisation align towards your strategy with joint ownership and ways of working.

That said you will need to have some key measures to monitor what you want to achieve and what you don't wish to disrupt. Here is a possible list of metrics you may want to consider. Realistically these should align to your strategic priorities:

- The degree to which the post-transaction financials meet the original business case or agreed changes there after

- A cultural assessment and alignment to the agreed strategy and plan (people, mission and vision) pre and post M&A

- Customer satisfaction and customer experience pre and post M&A

- Employee satisfaction pre and post M&A, as well as regretted attrition

- Operating model alignment to agreed plan and strategy and supporting economics and KPIs

- The degree the technology/digital objectives were delivered

- Lessons learnt register - what didn't go to plan or got broken, what would you do again and what you would do differently next time. Apply these learnings into future M&A and complex change activity.

- Management and mitigation of liabilities, including litigation risk (product, process, employees etc).

Success Insight 20. *Lastly, but most importantly... don't forget to say thank you!*

It takes hard work, focus, engagement, sponsorship and determination to get M&As right.

In a majority of cases you, your leadership team and change agents etc, will deliver the M&A on top of the day job. Recognising this and saying thank you is really important and goes a long way.

Celebrating early wins, innovative ideas, deliverables and key milestones all help to promote what good looks like, to accelerate change and demonstrate how people should be working.

Psychologically you also want to reward and recognise people for demonstrating the new behaviours and ways of working so people move towards them. In addition, recognising lessons learnt (both the positive and negative), helps people proactively get involved without a fear of making a mistake and being punished. They feel more able to try new things and get to grips with the new ways of working without retribution. It also helps reduce resistance to change, both emotionally and logically.

Keeping things simple, predictable and ensuring both formal and informal motivators are in place to reinforce the desired state, will help you accelerate the change and subsequent benefits. It also makes people feel better about the process.

You will then know when you've been successful, because you'll see it, hear it, feel it and people's willingness to get involved will be greater than their resistance.

Toolkit Overview

Toolkit Overview

The following diagram highlights some management tools you may want to consider within the stages of an M&A. Not a definitive list, but some I like:

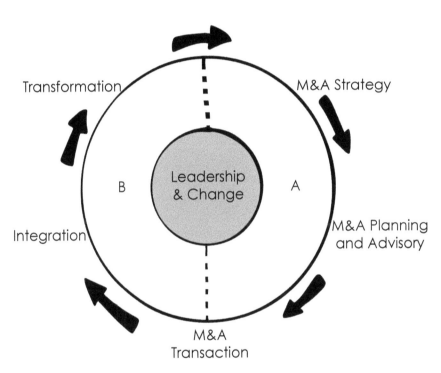

A. Combined proposition differentiation from a customer perspective; portfolio cannibalisation; competitor analysis; strategy development and supporting high-level plan; customer experience definition; organisation's combined purpose; combined culture assessment; leadership coaching, and talent management assessment.

B. Operational realism analysis; risk management and achievable realisation; existing programme/ project budget review; combined functional organisational design; retention planning; combined operational readiness; operational design principles; prisoner exchange; best of both analysis; end-to-end operational model to deliver the customer experience; change management communication plan.

About the Authors and Illustrators

Kerry Nutley is an experienced Leadership and Sales and Marketing transformation consultant, having worked for BT and Deloitte. As an HR Director Kerry supported BT Group during the EE and BT acquisition and led successful global M&A activity in BT Global Services. Kerry has a passion for complex change management leading through collaboration.

Adele Pickerill is an accomplished communications and engagement specialist, who has successfully led company-wide cultural, transformational and organisational change programmes in several high-profile companies. Adele has a track record of increasing employee engagement through impactful communications strategies, plans and campaigns, that support both the people and the business during times of complex change and M&A activity.

Zhuohan Shao is an international graphic design student from China. Enjoys the possibility of every cultural exchange. Studies about the design styles of different countries through travel, collection and reading.

Robert Hall is a graphic designer based in London, creating work through a mix of mediums such as editorial, printmaking and type design. Nominated for the Pengin Student design awards shortlist 2019.

Lightning Source UK Ltd.
Milton Keynes UK
UKHW022353141019
351598UK00006B/210/P